THOMAS ADÈS

These Premises Are Alarmed

for large orchestra

FABER  MUSIC

© 1998 by Faber Music Ltd
First published in 1998 by Faber Music Ltd
3 Queen Square London WC1N 3AU
Music processed by Christopher Hinkins
Cover design by S & M Tucker
Photograph © Tony Stone Images
Printed in England by Halstan & Co Ltd
All rights reserved

ISBN 0 571 51887 7

These Premises Are Alarmed was written for the Hallé Orchestra
during Thomas Adès's period as Composer-in-Association with them.
The first performance was given by the Hallé Orchestra conducted by
Kent Nagano at one of the Opening Concerts of the Bridgewater Hall,
Manchester on 12 September 1996

Duration: c.3 minutes

To buy Faber Music publications or to find out about the full range of titles available
please contact your local retailer or Faber Music sales enquiries:

Tel: +44 (0)171 833 7931
Fax: +44 (0)171 278 3817
E-mail: sales@fabermusic.co.uk
Website: http://www.fabermusic.co.uk

ORCHESTRA

3 piccolos (1 = flute)
3 oboes
3 clarinets (1 in B♭, 2 = A & bass clarinet, 3 in B♭ = E♭)
3 bassoons (3 = contrabassoon)

4 horns
3 trumpets (3 = piccolo in B♭)
2 tenor trombones (1 = bass trumpet in B♭)
bass trombone
bass tuba

percussion (4 players)
    1: crotales (shared with 2.) , marimba, 3 large roasting tins laid face down

    2: crotales (cf 1.), hi-hat cymbal, 4 field drums (large to small), 3 roasting tins (cf 1.),
    antique cymbals

    3: 4 gongs , glockenspiel, bass drum, small (kit) bass drum (flat), tam-tam

    4 : geophone, 2 wood blocks (high and very high), timpani (2 drums including),
    3 snare drums (medium to small), 6 inch roto-tom , 3 roasting tins (cf 1.)

harp
piano & celesta (five-octave) (1 player if possible)

strings (16.16.14.10.8. players) ★
★ double basses: at least half with C extensions

The score is notated in C

Orchestral parts available on hire from the publishers

PERFORMANCE NOTES

The notation ♩♩♩♩ means that the relevant group of notes must start slightly above the conductor's tempo and slow down to become gradually behind it. Where this rhythm appears next to another group of notes, it is to be treated as transitional in speed, from a faster to a slower group, for example:

The septuplet is a slowing down from the semiquavers to the triplets.

Where the arrow appears at the end of the group: ♩♩♩♩➚ an accelerando is implied.

Piano Preparation
Damp the following range with a strip of Blu-Tack® (or equivalent), placed on the strings between the player and the dampers:

Remove all the Blu-Tack at bar 48.

These Premises Are Alarmed

THOMAS ADÈS

A
B
Fl. 1
2
Picc.
3
staccatiss.
f staccatiss.
Ob. 2
pp staccatiss.
in B♭
Cl. in A
in E♭
p staccatiss.
Hn.
senza sord.
a2
Tpt. 2
Tbn.
Tba.
solo
Perc.
Crotales
struck
Gongs
l.v.
2 Very small woodblocks
Hp.
Pf. / Cel.
(Cel.)
(Pf.)
Piano
(Ped.)
Ped.
Vln.1 div.
2 desks
pizz.
arco, poco col legno
gli altri, div.
3 soli arco
ord.
Vln.2
gli altri div.
arco
Vla.
unis. (pizz.)
Vlc.
1 solo, arco
2 soli, arco
Db.

C
D
to Piccolo
Piccolo
f poss.
sim.
f come sopra
espr. agitato
p espr. agitato
solo
p come sopra
to Contrabassoon
mf col Fag.
stem fully inserted
Harmon mutes, stems fully inserted
Harmon mute, stem fully inserted
ossia
Hi-hat cymbal
Largest Snare drum
brushes
R.H.
L.H. swirl
F♮ A♮ B♭
C♭ E♭
E♯ A♯ D♭
Cel.
(Pf.)
Ped.
arco
unis. (pizz.)
arco, senza vib.
(pizz.)
unis. (pizz.)
div. a3
arco, poco sul pont.
pizz.
sul pont. acutissimo
3 soli
3 soli (pizz.)
gli altri
Fl. 1
Picc.
Ob.
in B♭
Cl. in A
in E♭
Bsn.
Hn.
Tpt.
Tbn.
Tba.
Perc.
Hp.
Pf. / Cel.
2 soli
Vln.1
gli altri
1 solo
Vln.2
gli altri div.
Vla.
Vlc. div. a3
Db.

39
F
Picc. 2
Ob. 2
in B♭
Cl. in A
in E♭
Bsn. 1 2
Cbsn.
Hn.
Tpt. 2
Tbn.
Tba.
Perc. 1
Marimba
Hp.
G♯
F♮ B♭
Pf.
Vln.1 div. a4
Vln.2 div. a3
Vla. div. a3
Vlc. div. a3
Db. div.
a2
pizz.
arco
IV
unis., pizz.
div. a4
unis.
div. a3
tutti Vlns:
s.p.
cresc.

* see Performance Note

♩ = 180
𝅗𝅥 = 90 accel.
𝅗𝅥 = ♩ =112 accel.
♩ = 144 accel.
♩. = ♩
101
M
Fl. 1
to Piccolo
Picc. 2 3
a2
Ob. 1 2.3
(a3)
cresc.
bells down
in B♭
solo
cresc.
Cl. Bass
solo
ff poss.
Bsn. 1 2
Cbsn.
Hn.
Tpt.
to Piccolo Trumpet
Tbn.
via sord., 1. to Bass Trumpet
Tba.
senza sord.
(ossia loco)
4 Field drums
Kit Bass drum (flat)
Bass drum
B.D.
f ma non troppo
Kit B.D.
Perc. 3
Timp.
Hp.
E♭ A♯
D♯
Pf.
Ped.
Vln.1
tutti unis.
Vln.2 div.
ord.
sul pont.
Vla.
unis., ord.
div.
unis.
2 soli
Vlc.
gli altri
Db. div.
pizz.
I solo, arco
ff poss.
arco